# Getting in Touch

**This book is to be returned on or before
the last date stamped below.**

DISCARDED

LIBREX

The Joseph Rowntree Foundation has supported this project as part of its programme of research and innovative development projects, which it hopes will be of value to policy makers and practitioners. The facts presented and the views expressed in this report, however, are those of the author and not necessarily those of the Foundation.

# Getting in Touch

Ways of working with people with severe
learning disabilities and extensive support needs

by Phoebe Caldwell

**RESEARCH *INTO* PRACTICE**

**RESEARCH *INTO* PRACTICE**

# Getting in Touch

A report on ways of working with people with
severe learning disabilities and extensive support needs

Phoebe Caldwell

**Published by:**

Pavilion Publishing (Brighton) Ltd.

8 St George's Place

Brighton

East Sussex BN1 4GB

Telephone: 01273 623222

Fax: 01273 625526

Email: Pavpub@pavilion.co.uk

First published 1996.

A Catalogue record for this book is available from the British Library.

ISBN 1 900600 05 6

**Editor:** Anna McGrail

**Cover, design and typesetting:** Stanford Douglas

**Printing:** York Publishing Services

# Contents

# Acknowledgements

This programme of work, teaching people who work with individuals with severe and profound learning disabilities, has been funded by the Joseph Rowntree Foundation. The author would like to express her thanks to the Trust and also to Dr Oliver Russell, Director of the Norah Fry Research Centre and Chairman of her Advisory Committee and all the members of that Committee who have supported her. She would also like to thank many students from different disciplines with whom she has worked and from whom she has learned a great deal.

In particular she would like to thank Margaret Flynn for her extensive editing, Geraint Ephraim for time spent mulling over ideas and answering questions, Carol Ouvery for her comments, Liz Byrne for her suggestions about 'changing the mode' of an intervention and Gunnar Birath for his reflection on 'assimilation time'.

Finally, she would like to thank all the support workers she has worked with and all the individuals who have shown her most of what she knows.

# Foreword

*Honorary Director*
*Norah Fry Research Centre*

I first met Phoebe Caldwell over twenty years ago when she was working in the occupational therapy department of a hospital for people with learning difficulties. Having become frustrated by the lack of appropriate equipment to use with people who were severely disabled by profound intellectual handicaps, and who were cut off from the world by visual problems or hearing deficits, she set about designing and making her own equipment. Phoebe began by creating large wooden jigsaws which could be easily assembled, even by those who had severe problems with the control of their fingers and thumbs. She recognised the need to use a variety of materials in the equipment she was making. As she became more accomplished as a carpenter and engineer so her designs became more adventurous. However, the success of her methods depended not only on her innovative equipment but also on the manner in which she approached the clients with whom she worked. She recognised the need to engage with her clients in ways that would draw them out of their isolation and withdrawal.

With generous support from the Mental Health Foundation, a videotape, *Reaching Out*, was made recording her work with a group of young men with severe challenging behaviour living on James Ward at Hortham Hospital in Bristol. Through her work on this project she was able to explore the nature of the relation-ship between the therapist and the person with profound disabilities. She became particularly interested in discovering how her techniques could enhance and facilitate the process of engagement between therapist and client. Her work became widely known and she was in great demand as a lecturer.

Phoebe soon recognised that her methods could also be applied in other contexts. Although many of those with whom she worked were confined to the back wards of mental handicap hospitals, there were others, equally isolated, who lived at home and attended their local day centre. Over the years she has shared her unique knowledge with many colleagues working in day centres and occupational therapy departments. However, concern was expressed that the knowledge, techniques and skills which she had accumulated over a period of twenty years should not be lost. Fortunately the Joseph Rowntree Foundation agreed in 1991 to fund a project, 'Skills and Development Therapy', which would enable Phoebe to teach her methods to a new generation of therapists. This proved to be a highly successful project. In her report on this work (*Reaching Out*, 1992) Alison Wertheimer described how therapists and day centre workers in all parts of England and Wales working with people with profound disabilities and sensory deficits were able to learn about Phoebe Caldwell's methods and apply them in their own work.

In order to consolidate the progress already achieved, and to train a critical mass of people skilled in working in this way, the Joseph Rowntree Foundation agreed in 1993 to fund an extension of the project. That extension ended in the summer of 1995 and in this report Phoebe Caldwell provides her own account of the ideas, philosophy and methods which she has developed over more than twenty years.

Phoebe argues that her approach depends on finding an appropriate 'language' through which to engage people with profound disabilities in meaningful interactions. Such a language need not be based on words, but may involve vibrations, sounds and touch. Many of the people with whom she and her students work have extreme support needs and live in impoverished and restricted social environments. Her success in reaching out to people living in the back wards of mental handicap hospitals or attending poorly equipped day centres is remarkable. In this report she reflects on her philosophy and writes about those with whom she has worked. She is a friend to many people with profound learning disabilities and sensory deficits who have missed out on opportunities to engage with the social world and an inspiration to the many therapists who wish to support their clients to have richer lives.

**Oliver Russell**,
1996.

# Introduction

There are some people with learning disabilities who confound the best efforts of their families and support staff to communicate with them. They may be variously described as 'profoundly disabled', 'multiply disabled', 'severely autistic', 'having learning disability' and, in addition, for some, as having 'challenging behaviour'. These labels, however, do not give any clues about developing ways of interaction between these people and their carers and their surroundings. Limited progress, or a reluctance to witness disappointment or failure, can close off many possibilities in the lives of these individuals as the following quotations suggest:

- 'We still don't know how to work with them.'

- 'We take them out shopping and on outings but they're not getting better.'

- 'It's difficult to work with people when you're not getting any feedback.'

These remarks have been gathered during a recent project funded by the Joseph Rowntree Foundation, to discover ways of working with people with whom meaningful communication seems difficult if not impossible. This project extended over four years. It involved teaching people from a wide variety of approaches and experience, such as management, occupational therapists, physiotherapists, psychologists, speech therapists, community nurses and social workers, and in some cases, untrained support personnel.

This report describes some aspects of the work. It shows that it is possible to reach and work together with the majority of people with extensive support needs by paying very close attention to these needs, both those that they share with all and also the very specific and individual demands resulting from the patterns of their behaviour.

The narratives included here involve the author, who is represented in the first person, the student on the course and the individual with whom they are working. Quite often they were observed by support staff and, for a limited period, sessions were watched by an observer appointed by the Joseph Rowntree Foundation (Wertheimer[1]).

Some significant developments in people's lives are described with the permission of those concerned. Names have been changed and some circumstances altered. A few incidents are included from work previous to the project where they are relevant and aid clarification. All the people involved were referred to the author because their support personnel were having severe problems in communicating and working with them.

## The shape of this report

The purpose of this report is to introduce the ideas investigated and developed before and during the period of funding by the Joseph Rowntree Foundation.

The starting point in **Section One** is a single premise based on a number of underlying ideas:

Some people who do not have language have learned to 'talk' to themselves in ways which seem to close off the possibility of communication with others. By using people's own 'language' it is possible to get in touch and engage their attention.

This is followed by an outline of course procedures and ideas followed.

**Section Two** provides a more detailed account of the ways in which it is possible to claim people's attention. It introduces a series of narratives which illustrate different aspects of the work.

**Section Three** looks at the many possible ways in which the use of personalised equipment makes it easier for support personnel and individuals with learning disabilities to get to know each other.

The fourth section, **Getting in Touch and Sharing Feelings**, considers the ways in which some people have become estranged from communication through circular speech patterns and behaviours which are cast as dysfunctional or 'disturbed'. This leads on to **Section Five, Working at an Appropriate Level**, which illustrates the underestimation-overestimation tension which can prevail in working with people with many support needs. The section closes with some summary points and an outline of the difficulties to be overcome.

**Section Six** considers the changes which have resulted from person-centred interventions and contains feedback from experienced support personnel, while **Section Seven** looks in detail at the design, use and range of equipment available.

# Section One
# Making Contact

Our training programme was based on a number of **underlying assumptions**:

1. **It is possible to engage with people who are apparently locked into stereotypic and repetitive behaviours**, for example, a complex series of finger movements, 'flicking' objects, or repetitive speech patterns.

2. **We are more likely to effect positive change in people's lives by improving their environments and patterns of care** if they are able to make a connection with what is going on around them.

3. **Engagement may lead to a form of 'language' based on touch, sound, vibration or movement.** This language may be so simple that we miss its potential.

4. **Some behaviours are self-stimulating and sometimes self-injuring but, by working through them, even they may act as pathways to get in touch.**

5. **It is crucial that we engage with people's language** and do not reject it on the grounds that it does not fit in with our ideas of what communication should be about.

6. **Some people find direct, face-to-face approaches intimidating.** In these situations it is necessary to find more indirect ways of working together.

7. Engagement, communication and exploration **can enrich our lives**.

The process of enacting these assumptions can be thought of as looking for a key to a room, as shown in *Figure 1* below.

### Figure 1

| 1 Looking for the 'correct' key, the one that fits. | → | Searching for the 'correct' stimulus, the one that a person 'recognises'. |
|---|---|---|
| 2 Opening the door. | → | Using the stimulus to attract the person's attention. |
| 3 Exploring the room. | → | Engaging with the person and building mutual confidence through listening and sharing. |
| 4 Looking out of the window. | → | Moving beyond ourselves to the worlds outside. |

## What the work looks like

The work which is the subject of this report focuses on finding ways to secure the attention of people who are often withdrawn, fearful or absorbed in repetitive behaviours.

The courses had no rigid syllabus but were developed from the particular circumstances surrounding the individuals with learning difficulties. Efforts were concentrated in interactive interventions which took place in locations where the person who was the focus of the work felt at ease. It will be seen that there was no such thing as a typical intervention.

Courses varied from two weeks to three months. As part of these, both the length of individual interactions and their number varied according to the individual and how quickly it was possible to gain their attention and establish a way of working to which they responded positively. Broadly, the approach adopted involved six elements.

1.  Learning from the student and support staff about an individual. This may include asking such questions as:

    - Is there a particular stimulus that the person is giving themselves?

    - Do they rock or scratch their hands?

    - Is there an object or activity that they are using to occupy their time?

    - How do you know about how they feel and interact with their world?

    - Is there a physical impairment blocking their ability to interact with the world outside?

    - Do they have visual or auditory impairments?

2.  Seeking to establish a helpful way of attracting the person's attention to which they respond positively. This may take place with the student and support staff present. We might ask such questions as:

    - By using a familiar stimulus, can we change a solitary activity into one which we can share together?

    - How can we move this person from the locked room of self-stimulus to one where they receive and recognise the stimulus as coming from outside themselves?

3.  Exploring with the student ways in which the process might be improved. This may mean asking questions such as:

    - How can we develop the exchange into a 'conversation' using stimuli the person recognises as a 'language'?

    - Is the person fearful or confused by face-to-face communication?

    - How might we present the stimulus indirectly?

    - Can we present the stimulus the person responds to in an even more fascinating form, by incorporating it into some kind of equipment to encourage them to reach out and explore?

4.  If we decide that personalised equipment would be helpful, it is designed and constructed with the student in a local workshop, using simple power tools and wood and/or plastic.

5.  We try out the equipment with the person who is the focus of our work and if necessary, it is modified or extended.

6.  Once a way of interaction has been established, discussions take place with support staff and their line managers, so that a consistent way of working may be sustained with the person.

# Section Two
# Getting Attention

Two significant approaches have informed the assumptions framing our way of working: intensive interaction* and working with stereotypic and repetitive behaviours.

## Intensive interaction

Ephraim[2] developed an extremely powerful way of working with people with profound learning disability and sensory loss and sometimes with people whose behaviour presents challenges. It involves joining in and imitating a person's repetitive and self-stimulating behaviour. For example, working with a person who is wriggling their fingers close to their eyes would involve placing my fingers also in this area, echoing what they are doing and joining in. This would present them with a dilemma: 'Here is a behaviour that I recognise but it comes from outside me.' The surprise which results typically secures attention.

A critical next task is to try and develop this **attention** into a 'conversation', a two-way **interaction**. As important as what is said and done, is what is conveyed by my attention:

- 'I am listening to you.'

- 'I am taking you seriously.'

---

* Nind and Hewett[3] have recently published a comprehensive and stimulating account of their use of Intensive Interaction with children at Harperbury Hospital School. This includes detailed descriptions of how the work is carried out and the background and processes involved.

- 'I value you.'

- 'I am here for you.'

The following nine narratives illustrate the key processes involved in securing people's attention. Each one includes lessons abstracted during work with people with learning difficulties, students and support personnel. The first four describe different types of intervention using **sound**, **sight**, **vibration** and **touch**, which arose from the individual's behaviour.

## 1. John

John is a very large man in his thirties, described as having severe disabilities, who lives in a group home. Because of his build and the nature of his challenging behaviour, he had a very large team of people working in shifts to support him. He liked to carry a range of objects which he could flick. He focused his whole attention on these 'flickers' and appeared to live in a world of his own. His days were filled with a series of activities chosen on the assumption that if he was not actually injuring himself or others, he was enjoying them. Observation suggested that he tolerated these occupations rather than enjoyed them.

During an initial meeting with support staff, when the range of his behaviours was being explored, John climbed on a trampoline and started to scratch the canvas with his fingernail. When I scratched back, he stopped and listened, waited to see if I would do it again. When I did, he replied. John and I then used this way of holding each other's attention, listening and answering, to build up a 'conversation'. He started to smile and laugh and changed from being self-absorbed and unreactive, becoming reciprocally responsive.

John's previous behaviours had two main characteristics: one was injuring himself; the other was tolerating activities in which he was essentially peripheral.

**His support team was encouraged to see John really joining in, in a way which he positively enjoyed, not only responding but also leading.**

For example, if I respond to his three scratches with three of my own, he knows I am listening to him. He can test this by varying the sounds he is making and seeing if I respond appropriately.

**The discovery of John's capacity to enjoy reciprocal activities led the support team to come up with their own ideas.**

They half-filled a lemonade bottle with water and rolled it back and forth across the table to him. It was not just that they had found something to amuse him but, because he enjoyed it, **they were getting positive feedback and were able to start building up a warmer relationship with him based on sharing enjoyment.** We begin to feel quite differently about people with whom we share laughter. ■

## 2. David

David is in his thirties and has recently moved from a long-stay hospital to a shared living scheme. He is described as having severe learning disabilities.

David had spent most of his life in an institution where he sat in a chair watching his fingers move close to his eyes, to the exclusion of anything going on round him.

The family with whom David lived were very creative and positive about him although it was very difficult to imagine how contact could be made with him. They said that although they were concerned that it might be thought age-inappropriate for him, they had copied his finger movements against a light to make animal shapes on the wall. They did this every evening.

**Their persistence paid off.** After three months, David started to join in and smile. This was the first response they had had from him. ■

## 3. Mary

Mary is in her thirties and has no sight. She has spent most of her life in an institution. Recently she moved into a home where she has a key-worker with whom she has a good relationship.

Mary had bits of string called 'things'. She did not like them being touched and scratched me when I tried to work with them with her.

She also stamped and kicked furniture. Although she sometimes initiated an approach to her key-worker, mostly she rejected touch and scratched. She was regarded as being extremely difficult to motivate and interact with.

When Mary walked into a room she walked round it, kicking each piece of furniture and then lay down in the middle and drummed her heels on the floor. It seemed to me that she was using sound as a locating system. Her habit of kicking furniture was her way of establishing contact with the world about her. **Vibration and sound were her language.**

In order to make contact with her, I also

stamped on the floor. She stopped drumming her heels and paid attention. An exchange of stamps followed and then she stood up and stamped round the room. I followed her, stamping, and she started to smile. She then lay down in the middle of the room and waited. Starting at one corner, I stamped towards and over her, lifting my feet over her prone body. Mary laughed. She got up and started 'bumping' me round the room. From a situation where, twenty minutes before, she had been isolated and miserable, **by using her 'language', we were able to make conversation and enjoy each other's company.**

In another session, Mary had taken her shoes off and was shuffling on the floor. She did not respond to my stamping. It was only when I copied her lead and made the same sound that she began to respond. Later on we made contact through tapping a tin. It was Mary who liked to decide exactly which sound should be used to 'talk' to me, she liked to be in control. ■

### 4. Gary

Gary is in his twenties, has no sight and has severe cerebral palsy. One arm is in splints to prevent his pushing his hand into his mouth and throat compulsively. He lives in a group home and likes listening to music to which he rocks. Otherwise he had been regarded as impossible to motivate, spending most of his time sitting in his room.

**Gary tapped his wrist and it had been thought that this was an indication that he was becoming upset. In fact he responded well to using this stimulus as a way of building up conversation.** He began to smile and laugh when support staff did this with him and during regular subsequent sessions, they have been able to remove his

splint and he has made no attempt to return his hand to his mouth. When I met him six months later, he was able to last for a period of two hours without the splint but with someone touching him occasionally. ■

The following narrative, **Roger**, illustrates that repetitive behaviour may involve a sequence of movements. For an intervention to be successful, it may be necessary to join in all parts.

### 5. Roger

Roger appeared completely withdrawn and scratched the palm of his left hand, alternating this with using his left hand to clasp his right. When I joined in and scratched his left hand, he seemed to notice but continued to try and clasp his right hand.

**It wasn't until I joined in both parts of the sequence, — scratch — clasp — scratch — clasp — that he became fascinated and started to smile and wait for my intervention.** He responded, raising his head from its customary sunken position and smiling at me. ■

The next narrative, **Andrew**, shows that some people may vary their established behaviours to see if their lead is being followed.

### 6. Andrew

Andrew presented as very anxious and spent his days darting from one place to another. He was said to be disturbed by strangers but responded when I copied him rubbing his cheek. He stopped his agitated wandering and answered me, at first with the same gesture, and then with a whole range of hand and arm movements not in his normal repertoire. He waited to see if I got them right and when I did he laughed. ∎

It will be recalled that the element of surprise is critical. This needs to be maintained by introducing variations, for example, by altering the rhythm or the way in which a sound is presented. The next two narratives illustrate how surprise is maintained by presenting stimuli in different ways.

## 7. Kate

Kate is partially sighted. She spent most of her time rocking against a wall. Each time she banged, I squeezed an accordion sharply, echoing her rhythm. After a short interval, she started to smile and turned to me from her banging. She examined the accordion and started to share pressing the buttons with me.

**Her attention had been diverted from the self-injuring behaviour to a shared activity** which we were able to enjoy together. ∎

## 8. Bill

Bill used to rock his body most of the time. He was totally absorbed, to the extent that my copying him went unnoticed, but when I echoed his rocking by running a stick up and down a length of corrugated tube in time to him, he started to look at me, laugh and reach out with his hands. ∎

The next narrative, **Polly**, demonstrates that if a person feels uncomfortable if they are too close to other people, we may have to find ways of working at a distance.

## 9. Polly

Polly used to spend a lot of her time making crying noises and ran away upstairs when I sat beside her and copied her. I did not move, but continued to echo the noises which came from her bedroom where she had retreated. After a while, she came down and put her head round the corner, watching me. When I looked up, she retired again. Still **I did not move, allowing her to choose the distance**, but continued to echo her. After about ten minutes she came and sat beside me and, from then, we were able to **use her sounds to start a conversation**. Then she took the lead in a series of hand movements, something she had not been known to do before. ∎

From the detail of the preceding narratives some points merit re-stating.

- Self-stimulatory and repetitive behaviours can get in the way of communication.

- Although it might be claimed that a person with very extensive support needs 'is not doing anything', we all focus on something, even if it is as simple as a breathing rhythm.

- People exhibit surprise when the stimulus that they are used to giving themselves comes from a source outside themselves.

- Interventions have to be very specific and tailored to people's established behaviour. The more closely the stimulus echoes a person's own behaviour, the greater the likelihood of obtaining a positive response.

## Working with stereotypic and repetitive behaviours

Most of the people we have discussed so far have been absorbed by behaviours which centre on physical stimuli they are giving themselves using their own bodies by, for example, scratching, making noises and flapping. However, there are other people, many of whom are diagnosed as having 'autistic features', who focus their whole attention on particular external objects and no variation is acceptable. Usually they do not want to share these or take turns.

The next two narratives — **Rodney** and **Sarah** — deal with people whose attention is focused on spinning objects.

One way of working creatively with this, is to inundate the person with more of the object than they can physically control. This opens up the possibility of negotiations such as:

- 'Which is yours?'
- 'Which can I have?'
- 'Which is mine?'
- 'Can I have this one?'
- 'Shall we put them in a box?'

These narratives describe the difficulties encountered when people fear their precious things are going to be taken from them.

### 10. Rodney

Rodney was fascinated by objects which could be spun. He twirled objects in a repetitive way to the exclusion of social interaction. He was offered a large number of different sorts of objects such as cones, discs and short pieces of tube in a box. There were more than he could handle. **The student was able to use the surplus to negotiate and offer alternatives.**

Gradually Rodney began to pay more attention to the student's part in the interaction — she was allowed to help him stack the tubes and when one became wedged inside a cone, he accepted a rod from her to dislodge it. He interacted with her and used the objects in a wider variety of ways than he was accustomed to. ■

### 11. Sarah

Sarah was also interested in 'spinners'. We made a number of discs and gave them to her in a box. She started to use them at once, and when prompted, handed them round for us to spin as well. From being a solitary activity in which she was absorbed 'in her own world', it became a basis for social interaction — an activity through which she could relate to others. However, it was easy for her to become overexcited, so her key worker explored limited sessions of a few minutes at a time. It was possible that her rising excitement initiated sensory overload so she could no longer handle even things she readily enjoyed. ■

The next narrative — **George** — demonstrates how a man was able to share his interest when he was given more space in which to work.

### 12. George

George is described as having 'severe autism'; he draws endless pictures of houses and road plans on A4 paper. He will not allow anyone to join in. I offered him a very large sheet torn from an industrial roll. This allowed him more space and he didn't feel so threatened when I started to make additions. He became quite relaxed about 'taking turns' with the pen and seemed interested in my road cones and traffic lights. He clearly recognised them as being appropriate. When the student and I added model cars to his road plans and drove them round, he was less happy, until we added a car park where they could be contained. His attention was so caught by this interactive activity that he was quite peaceful and engaged even while waiting for lunch, a time which he normally finds so hard that he self-injures, banging his head. He allowed himself to be last in the queue. His mother commented that he seemed to be more alert and engaged all evening: he had obviously enjoyed himself. It was clear that, simply giving him a larger area to work in, albeit with the boundaries he required, reduced his anxiety and made it possible for him to share. ■

### In conclusion

- Stereotypic and repetitive behaviours keep people in carefully maintained, safe places.

- It is possible to find creative ways of assisting people to look outwards from these behaviours.

- People need opportunities to retreat if they appear overwhelmed; for example, by negotiating distance and by reducing the time of interventions.

# Section Three

# Engagement Through Personalised Equipment and Interventions

Having found a way of attracting a person's attention — through touch, sound, sight, movement or vibration — it is sometimes helpful to incorporate the particular stimulus to which the person responds into personalised equipment.

This is best thought of as **a means of helping two people to work together**. The use of attractive materials helps draw attention towards the task and makes it more interesting. Above all, however, personalised equipment is a means by which two people can engage in a shared activity in an enjoyable way.

Once again, a series of narratives illustrate the ways in which equipment may be used to deepen people's engagement.

### David

#### Continued from Narrative 2

David's family had used his finger movements to develop a game to which he responded (see page 6). I was asked to devise ways of extending his experiences, particularly during the winter when it was difficult to take him outside. I introduced him to a mirror with holes through which our fingers could be wriggled, and also a box with holes through which fingers could be pushed. In this case he was asked to hold a transparent cup to 'catch my finger' when it appeared. At first he needed prompting but soon grasped the idea and was laughing as he tried to put the cup over my finger before it disappeared. From being difficult to engage, he enjoyed an interaction with someone else. ■

### 13. Jeff

Jeff is partially sighted and has severe learning disabilities. He sat in a chair all day with his head tilted back, rubbing his hair with his hands. His support workers found it impossible to make contact with him. It was thought that it might help him if he had some idea of himself and to this end they wanted to try and get him to look at himself in a mirror but he resisted their attempts to persuade him to do so. It seemed that the first problem was his position — he needed to bring his head down instead of looking at the ceiling in order to see the mirror.

We made a mirror which had a 'mat' of Astroturf at one end. It was positioned on his lap, with the Astroturf nearest him, and his hands were brought down and placed on it. At first he tried to return his hands to his head but gradually kept them down and started to explore the prickly springy texture by himself. At this stage, it was tempting to allow ourselves to be side-tracked into seeing if there were other surfaces he would enjoy, **but there is a danger that glimpses of such promise can lead to fast-forwarding the introduction of a further stage, without attending to what can be learned from the present one**. It was important for us not to rush on but to watch carefully and share what he was doing. His fingers continued to explore the Astroturf and then found the mirror. This was quite a different surface. His fingers started to move backwards and forwards from the rough spiky surface to the cool smooth one, two different textures.

We learned that he was interested in making comparisons — information we could have missed if we had been speculating about other possibilities and also information vital to extending his experiences. By now, his head had followed his hands down and he was beginning to sneak the odd glance at himself in the mirror. ■

with different tactile materials, in particular, Astroturf. At first, Ian allowed his hands to be placed on the Astroturf. In the following session he knelt up and started bending over and examining the boxes. By the third time he was smiling and engaged with the boxes for twenty minutes. He started to turn round and laugh at the student who he could feel kneeling beside him, sharing enjoyment with her, a very important stage in building relationships and making friends.

The student commented that although she had been working with Ian for years on behavioural programmes she had never seen him respond and interact like this before. That was two years ago. His parents say that he has 'come on' since then. He is more alert and uses his fingers to explore. He does not lash out as he used to and is more friendly and trusting with people. ■

### 14. Ian

Ian is in his twenties. He lives at home and attends a day centre for people with special needs. He has profound learning disabilities, physical disabilities and very little sight. When the student and I first saw him he enjoyed rolling about on the floor but this was very difficult for his family, as he tended to pull furniture on top of himself. Much of his time was spent strapped in a wheelchair facing a corner so that he did not grab things. On the floor he just rolled away from any approach. Occasionally he 'lashed out' at people.

Time spent with Ian started on the floor. We found that when the palms of his hands were tickled he stopped rolling away and paid attention. The student designed a piece of equipment which consisted of two horizontally mounted rotating boxes, which allowed both his hands to be engaged at once. The sides of the boxes were covered

### 15. Peter

Peter presented as extremely difficult to work with. He spent his time restlessly pacing a large hall, licking the walls in three specific places. If his routine was interfered with he became distraught and attacked his support staff, biting, scratching and hitting. He reacted to interference as though his life was threatened. Clearly, any stimulus that was going to attract and hold his attention needed to be very powerful indeed for him. I sat at a table and spun a flanged box covered with mirror which turned round a horizontal bar. As soon as Peter noticed this, he came over and sat down, starting to spin the box for himself. He was obviously fascinated by it and would have continued endlessly. Although this was an improve-ment on his previous behaviour, there was no interaction with me. He was still in a private world. I looked for an activity which would continue to provide him with the stimulus he recognised and enjoyed — spinning — but one that would involve us both.

I offered him a puzzle in which discs had to be moved from one end of a bar to the other, at the same time turning them to pass them over a series of pegs. The discs could be made to spin. He focused on this at once but needed help to get them over the obstacles. He allowed me to place my hands on his in order to do this. ■

## 16. Luke

Luke has 'severe symptoms of autism' and experienced direct intervention as extremely confrontational and threatening. He was very withdrawn and locked into rituals. He could do jigsaws but in an automatic way without regard to the pictures. Having watched him walking on paving stones without treading on the cracks, I designed a game to work with him through a pattern I thought he would recognise. A large piece of card was ruled into four inch squares with heavy black lines. I placed it on the floor in front of him and tried to flick black two-inch discs into the squares so they didn't touch the lines — they were then 'safe'. He watched out of the corner of his eye. When I asked if he would like to play, he said, 'NO'. I then asked if I might play again to which he also said, 'NO'. I left it for a minute or two and then asked again if I might play. After a few more 'No's, he grunted, a sound more like 'Yes' so I took this as permission to play. After this, he took control of the game, saying 'Yes' or 'No' as to whether or not I might play. As yet he would not join in.

After a while, the game was moved to the table and Luke was persuaded to leave his chair and join in. He began to work interactively through the non-threatening

pattern of lines and squares that he recognised as 'safe'. ■

## 17. Jack

Jack has autism. He spent a lot of time running around his garden. Sometimes he came and tapped the window but ran away if approached. It appeared that he wanted to communicate but could not manage direct interaction. We decided to try using a transparent plastic screen with him, to enable him to come to us without feeling threatened.

The first time, the student sat with it held up on her lap and tapped it. He kept looking round the door to observe what was going on and eventually came into the room and walked round her, looking at it.

In the following session, the screen was on the floor. Jack came into the room, picked it up, placed it on her lap and tapped it, laughing.

Jack could manage to come close if there was a boundary and it was presented in a way that he recognised, a 'window' to tap. ■

## 18. Steve

Steve lives in a group home. When I first met him he was in a long-stay hospital. He had severe challenging behaviour and was violent. He has severe learning disability and only has sight in his left eye.

All Steve's attention seemed to be focused on his left foot. He constantly drew attention to it and it was difficult to interest him in anything else. Sometimes it was possible to massage this foot and then work with him, i.e., we first paid attention to the place where he seemed to be centred before we asked him to 'do' something. The first task was to catch his attention so that he was absorbed in the equipment and therefore less likely to be violent.

I used a row of very brightly coloured and attractive pegs to be put in holes, trying to get him to scan, i.e. to turn his head from left to right so that he could see what was going on. Over a period of months, seeing him once a week, but with the help of support staff in between, I gradually moved the pegs on the table from his left to the right. **He learned to follow them and to turn his head. He was able to transfer this new skill unaided to other activities** such as pulling the toilet flush, which he had previously been unable to do, as it was on the right-hand side and he had not been able to see it. At this point his behaviour started to improve. While this was partly because he had moved house and his environment had improved, it also seemed to be a consequence of being more aware of what was going on on his right-hand side, so he was less vulnerable to being frightened by unexpected approaches from that side. Also, support personnel were more attuned to the importance of consistency in approaching Steve so that they did not invoke a fear reaction.

## Gary

### Continued from Narrative 4

Gary is blind and has cerebral palsy. He was only able to grasp with one hand and his other arm and hand were becoming rigid. We designed a piece of equipment for him which consisted of a bar attached at both ends to a loop of rope which I could hold on to. His hands were placed on the bar which was covered with corrugated tube and felt interesting. At first he only held on with his left hand but gradually he learned to hold on with his right hand as well. He enjoyed it

when support staff gently tugged on the rope so he knew they were there. It enabled him to straighten his rigid arm.

Although Gary was able to respond for short periods, he appeared to retreat into himself and lose interest. At the end of this period he would sigh, and after the sigh he was able to continue. Birath[4] pointed out that it is important when interacting with people with profound disabilities to allow them time to 'assimilate' input, and that the end of this 'assimilation time' is often marked by a sigh. This observation was very helpful when pacing work with Gary. It ensured that we did not force the pace beyond that which he could manage. ■

## 19. Mike

Mike is in his forties and has brain damage as the result of an accident. Before this, although he had no sight and probably little effective hearing, he had above average intelligence. It was difficult to assess how much brain damage there was because of problems of communicating with him. Support workers tried writing on his hands but he tired after two or three letters and became angry. He seemed depressed and rejected approaches. He spent much of his time sleeping. It was almost impossible to motivate him to do anything and difficult to tell whether he could not do it or just did not want to. He was able to pour and drink a cup of tea without spilling a drop.

Although Mike could speak, his disabilities made it impossible for support staff to get through to him. He could not manage to learn sign language at this stage.

Writing on his hand did not work as it was:

- temporary, as the letters disappeared when they had been made;

- passive; and

- different support workers did it differently.

We made wooden letters, three-and-a-half inches high, which Mike could feel with the palm of his hand and trace with the forefinger of the other hand, a movement similar to 'writing' that letter and involving motor memory. The letters did not disappear, they were available for him to check up on.

In consultation with a psychologist, we decided to start with 'NO' and 'OK' to see if Mike could cope with the system. The two letters were joined to make a unit. After two days he asked where the 'YES' was. From then on, communication was established and has continued to get easier. He now has small letters on a portable board. He sometimes is able to manage on his own in the pub. From being totally isolated, he is able to interact with people. Further, he has learned to do his own cooking and he manages with much reduced support. ■

The next narrative illustrates how something as abstract as time was made more concrete for one man, **Alex**. He used to ask over and over again questions such as: 'When's Pete on?', 'When's the bus coming?', 'When am I going on holiday?' Replies never satisfied him because they had no meaning, as they did not link into any pattern he could grasp.

## 20. Alex

Alex was very distressed when he heard the word 'holiday'. He thought that it meant that others were going away and he was going to be left behind. I gave him a modified year planner — the months were cut in strips and mounted on a dark sheet of card so that it was clear which way the days were to be crossed off. We stuck a picture of suitcases onto the date of his holiday. This gave his

support workers a way of negotiating with him in a way that he could easily understand. They could show him where his holiday was and where he was now and the time-space in between. This simplified calendar reduced his anxiety and he no longer lost his temper with people who were not able to tell him what he needed to know.

This type of intervention can be equally well designed for week or day calendars, or in a different format for short periods of time such as two hours. It gives an opportunity to convert a situation that is difficult to work with into an interaction where negotiation is possible and the individual is reassured. ■

The following narrative shows that colour laser photocopying — enlarging colour photographs — offers a good way of working with people with a confused self-image in a creative manner. Small photographs can be enlarged, even to life size. A4 and A3 enlargements can be used to great effect in life history books and to make jigsaws of individuals.

## 21. Laurence

Laurence was confused and called himself by his brother's name 'Simon'. A photograph was taken of him and Simon, sitting beside each other on a wall, and this was enlarged to A4. This was cut into a two-piece jigsaw so that Laurence could see and name himself, both with his brother and separately. His confusion ceased. ■

## 22. Sharon

Sharon is an older woman who has spent much of her life in institutions and has recently moved to a group home. She hits herself, often for no apparent reason and it is difficult to interest her in any activities. Sometimes she plays scales up and down on a keyboard.

When I played low notes on an accordion, she put her hands on it and felt the movement and vibration. She started to laugh. Whereas playing the keyboard was something she did on her own, the session with the accordion was a new situation, one of relating to me. Not only did she laugh then but, when we met shortly after the session, she looked straight at me and laughed again, sharing the joke and pleasure that we had had together. It was not only the notes she had enjoyed as she played the keys, but the mutual interaction, the human bit. What had originally been an isolated self-stimulus was transformed into having fun with someone else, not only at the time they were doing it, but also following on from that, in recollection. Even if, as at this time, it was very short term, the pleasure had passed from, 'something that is happening now' to memory — it was getting built in. She had a new way of reacting to a stranger, something she normally found difficult. This had been done by focusing her attention on a pattern of sound that she recognised and could share. ■

The preceding narratives indicate that the use of personalised equipment has several benefits:

- for people who are very withdrawn it may be advantageous to present stimuli in a more compelling form than that which they are used to, so that they want to reach out and explore the source

- games can be used in ever-widening ways to help people experience affinity and relationship with others

- working face-to-face may be too demanding for some people; it is less so if we are sharing an activity, as attention can be focused, not so much on each other, as on what we are doing together

- we can use the way of working that a person finds interesting, to explore and work through physical problems, such as helping them to learn to grasp or use both hands together when they may otherwise not be willing to do this

- people with severe visual impairment need extra stimulus; personalised equipment can help provide this, whether it be helping them to learn to turn their heads, to make better use of the sight they have, or to aid communication, or to provide the additional tactile input they require

- personalised equipment is adapted to the immediate needs of an individual; for example, a number of people with cerebral palsy have communication systems which are under-used as their communication boards are too large to fit into their wheelchairs. Designing a book which fits in the chair, with stiff pages which are flanged and easy to turn, means the system is always to hand.

Against these benefits, some caution has to be introduced:

**There is danger of individualised equipment being viewed as an end in itself. Its power to engage attention and facilitate interaction is lost if it is allowed to become a means of solitary occupation.**

# Section Four

# Getting in Touch and Sharing Feelings

Engaging with the perplexing personal worlds of people with extensive support needs rarely features in their Individual Programme Plans or reviews. Although they have learned to 'talk' to themselves, the ways in which they do this seem to close off the possibility of communication with others. For some, the need to preserve a sense of privacy may present as risk aversion: for example, a repetitive, circular speech pattern to which a person constantly returns. Such individuals may become isolated, as support staff give up using speech as a way to communicate with them. It is easier to focus on teaching them skills than to empathise with how they feel or how the world appears to them.

The next two narratives demonstrate ways of working with women who used speech in such a way that it hindered rather than facilitated communication.

## 23. Pat

Pat uses a tight spiral of repetitive sentences about pop stars from the sixties and people whom she knew in the past. She gets upset and may start hitting if efforts are made to enlarge the content of her speech.

Finding a way of infiltrating Pat's speech patterns in a non-threatening way was the first task. Previous interventions had shown that simply 'staying with' the questions and continuing to answer them resulted in Pat becoming calmer. However, it was easy to become trapped in the cycle and there seemed to be no possibility of change.

An alternative was to explore the stereotype of pop stars in a way that was not dependent on language. Photographs of her favourite pop star were inserted between a white clip-board and an acetate sheet. A white-board pen was used to draw round the image and then the photograph was removed, leaving an outline which she was invited to amend: for example, 'Add the hair'. Pat watched all this, fascinated, then picked up the pen and joined in the drawing. She also started to speak in a more relevant way. In a subsequent session, she suddenly used the board in a different way, scribbling all over her drawing and clearly expressing great anger. After this, she began to ask to go shopping and to buy a particular item, something she had not previously done.

It is difficult to understand how these patterns of speech arise, but it could be that they have their origin in the need to protect the person from feelings that they find unbearable. It is very important that if we alter the mode of intervention so as to get close to a person, we recognise that they may feel vulnerable. If there is any sign of anxiety, we need to be prepared to withdraw, returning to the mode in which the person feels safe. ■

### 24. Linda

Linda used stereotypic speech patterns to protect herself. These centred on a town with which she was familiar. She was extremely nervous about being in the local workshop, as she is with all new places. Initially, instead of ignoring or trying to over-ride her single repeated topic, I explored it with her and began to get answers that were wider than those she normally gave. I went on to acknowledge her nervousness, reflecting on how strange it is in new places with new people. It was only after this, after she had reassured herself by talking about 'her place' and her feelings, that she was able to gather strength to begin a new activity, albeit unrelated to her town. As we were in the workshop, I asked her if there was anything she would like me to make for her using power tools and she said she would like an animal, a cow. When I had cut it out, she indicated that she would like to try. The student put his hands over hers and together, they used the jigsaw to cut plywood. She shouted with excitement, 'I've done it, I've cut!' This stream of confidence spilled into her conversation, and she asked to return the following week, even though she had been seen as someone who found it 'difficult to make choices'. ■

Sometimes people feel angry and frustrated about their inability to connect and deal with emotions common to all of us. This is illustrated in the following narrative, **Ron**.

### 25 Ron

Ron is in his late thirties and was described as having 'severely challenging behaviour'. Both 'time out' and sedation were familiar service responses. One aspect of his unpredictable outbursts was that, although normally articulate, he was unable to say why he attacked people, particularly his mother. He was distressed if asked and really seemed not to know why he did it. Based on the assumption that the feelings which triggered the attacks were too hard for him to look at, a board game was designed for him. The layout was of the 'Monopoly' type, i.e. with squares around the edge of the board. These squares were situations rather than places. Each had a question relating to that situation with alternative answers, the outcome to which was decided by throwing dice, that is, by chance.

Each player had a 'Goody' and a 'Baddy' who, starting from 'Go', moved round the board in opposite directions. (This was based on the premise that all of us have parts of ourselves who behave like 'baddies' sometimes. The 'goody' and 'baddy' pieces were deliberately stereotyped cartoon-type figures.)

If a 'Goody' and a 'Baddy' landed on the same square, a special die was thrown to decide which answer the player gave. Either player had an equal chance of getting it 'wrong'. For example, Goody and Baddy, coming from opposite ways round the board, both land on the dentist square. They are afraid. The question asks, do they (a) tell the dentist about their fear and ask for a pain killing injection? Or (b) bite him?

The aim of the game was to enable Ron to recognise, talk about and even laugh at feelings, mine and his. For example, I wanted to help him understand that it was 'all right' and normal for him to feel angry, frustrated and frightened, that it was part of ordinary life that he shared with all people. To this end, it was essential in designing the game that there was no moral loading.

Work continued with this and other games over a period of months. Ron moved from a position of being unable to account for his violence to that of stating, 'You know, I'm not going to get better while I feel so angry'. I said I thought this was very important. Later on, he was able to tell me that he was beginning to feel upset and was able to grip my hands, instead of grabbing my hair, as he had formerly. ■

Some people find a direct approach very threatening. Writing in her book *Nobody Nowhere*, Williams[5] describes her experience of autism and how she found eye contact and direct speech physically painful. In such a situation it may be better to adopt **a deliberately indirect approach**, that is, not looking at the person and talking *about* them rather than *to* them, as the following narrative shows.

### 26. Paula

Paula has 'severe autism and challenging behaviour'. Much of her time is spent in her room which she decorates with scraps of paper torn from magazines, which she licks and sticks to the walls. She does not respond easily to interventions, particularly from strangers, and is liable to destructive outbursts. When I first saw her, she was sitting on her bed twiddling her hair. She avoided my gaze. Bearing this in mind I stood by the door, twiddling my own hair, looking away from her out of the window and said, 'If I was doing this, after a bit I should want to brush my hair and if I wanted to brush my hair I should put my hairbrush on the bed'. Paula put her hairbrush on the bed immediately and after I had brushed her hair and continued chatting indirectly, Paula hugged me. Next day, using the same indirect technique, the student encouraged her to make a cup of tea, an activity she had previously been

reluctant to help with. She used the same indirect technique and the session ended with Paula embracing her. ■

Paula wanted to make contact but found direct approaches too painful. She was able to respond very positively to interventions that did not make these demands on her.

Sometimes it is possible to enable an individual to explore their feelings even if they have limited or no speech. The next three women, whose behaviours were described as 'very disturbed', all responded dramatically to images of babies.

### 27. Janie

Janie spent much of her time pulling out her hair. She was often restrained from self-injury. On an occasion when she had been screaming for some hours, she was shown the image of a baby. She stopped screaming, leant forward and put out her hands and said, 'Ahh-h.' She went on to hug the 'baby' and wiped its face with a cloth. ■

### 28. Ellen

Ellen was violent and she smeared her faeces. She was thought to be impossible to engage until I tried working with her with simple jigsaws and pictures of babies. The images of babies allowed her to explore a range of feelings to which she did not normally have access. In time, Ellen ceased to reject or grab me when I arrived. She welcomed me and led me to the room where we worked together. I became someone she trusted. ■

## 29. Ann

Ann, who is in her thirties and lives in a community home, sat curled up in a chair. Apart from her key support worker, she hit out at people who came too close. We introduced the images of babies to her and support staff worked with them with her intensively for a fortnight. During this time she started to relate to people in a different way, putting out her arms to welcome them, including kissing her sister when she visited, something she had never done before. ■

Sometimes people feel very protective towards objects they regard as precious. Behaviour we call 'challenging' can arise out of our failure to recognise this need.

People may desperately try to hold on to these objects, the qualities of which are not readily apparent to others. Many people in service settings have nowhere to keep such things, which may be deemed inappropriate, sometimes being removed and restored in the name of 'punishment' and 'reward' for behaviour.

Endorsing the importance of favoured objects by providing a place to hold them, facilitates the processes of growth and moving on, as the next narratives of **Jim** and **Frank** show.

## 30. Jim

Jim is in his late thirties and is described as having severe learning disabilities. He lived at home until his parents could no longer manage. He was admitted to long-stay hospital care with 'clinical depression and challenging behaviour' which took the form of wrecking furniture, eating small bits of plastic and being unable to relate in any

positive way to other people. He was frequently restrained and was so heavily sedated that he found it difficult to walk without falling over. He had no effective use of language.

Jim was transferred to another residence where the patterns of his behaviour were examined closely. We focused attention on why he was doing what he was doing and how he felt. We realised that he was breaking furniture to obtain bits of plastic. Since these were taken away from him, he was eating them in order to keep them. He then broke more furniture to get more plastic.

In order to try to break this cycle, I suggested to him that we should make a box in the workshop, so that he could keep his pieces of plastic safe. He was fascinated by all the processes, particularly the use of power tools with their interesting vibration.

Jim enjoyed his sessions in the workshop. After the first one, he went back to his residence and said, 'Box', when he was asked what he had been doing.

When the box was finished and Jim realised that it was his and he could use it to keep his bits in, he stopped wrecking furniture and also stopped eating plastic. He began to express himself more in words and to relate to others in his group, to the extent of using rubber balls in games with them, instead of biting them to pieces. Since there was no longer a need to sedate him, he no longer staggered when he walked and became extremely good at a modified form of table tennis. From being a very depressed man, he could often be heard laughing.

X-rays taken before and after our work together showed an improvement from a stomach full of foreign bodies to just one.

Jim went on to join an evening class which he attended with his support worker. With great pride he showed me a wooden joint he had made. He now attends day-services unaccompanied. He still uses his box. Recently, after several years had elapsed, we met and he took me to his room to see what he had in it now. He uses it to store his collection of rubber balls. ■

### 31. Frank

Frank liked screws so much that he obtained them by removing them from furniture. Doors fell off their hinges and legs off tables. We suggested that he should make a box for his screws. We took great care, with his help, to glue the screws in with Araldite so that his box 'wouldn't fall to pieces'. He poked the glue into the screw-holes himself on the end of a matchstick. He made no attempt to unscrew his box and was proud of it, fetching it to show visitors. By this means, a process that was destructive, started to become constructive. ■

Making boxes together to hold objects serves a number of benefits:

- it endorses the significance of people's precious objects

- making something together adds to feelings of self-worth

- it provides an opportunity for shared 'hands-on' work.

# Section Five
## Working at an Appropriate Level

The narratives outlined in earlier sections demonstrate that it is always possible to explore new ways of getting in touch with people; and that these can effect significant changes in people's behaviours, albeit to different degrees. The *under*-expectation which is so often associated with teaching people with learning disabilities may well disadvantage people with extensive support needs. Paradoxically, however, these people are also vulnerable to *over*-expectation and being bombarded with a range of sensory stimulation. In turn, even experienced support staff are deceived and view such people in limiting ways. This is particularly true of some people with extensive sensory impairment with whom it is difficult to establish communication, who have withdrawn into a 'safe' world of self-stimulation and little mobility.

Most of the information we receive is visual and too often the effects of poor sight and blindness are underestimated. Similarly the impacts of deafness on people with limited understanding and often sensory losses are insufficiently understood. Some people have learned that sitting in a chair or standing in a corner is safer, if experience has taught them that when they move, something or someone may hurt them.

### 32. Jeff

Jeff has no sight and some speech, described as 'an indecipherable mutter'. He spent his days rocking in the corner of a room. He hated to be touched. On a 'good' day he attended a day centre, where he might have threaded one bead. He presented as a person with very severe learning disability. Enquiry elicited that at one time he had enjoyed trips to the beach with his mother when she had been alive. He was taken to a shingle beach on a wild day so he could hear the waves crashing. Because he could not see, he had to hold on. After two hours, he was climbing over the sea defences, laughing. When a member of his support team wondered what they should do next, he said cheerfully, 'Go for a lager?'

Jeff had been offered activities at a totally inappropriate level, both at his day centre and in his group home. In fact, he had withdrawn from situations that to him were sensorally confusing, so that he presented as a man much less able than he was. When he was given a very strong stimulus, that resonated with his history, he responded in a totally unanticipated way. ■

**Norah**, described in the narrative overleaf, required an approach at a very simple level.

### 33. Norah

For many years Norah has sucked a lump she makes of screwed-up plastic, over which she regurgitates. She strongly resisted efforts to substitute for this activity. She was persuaded to part with the plastic ball in exchange for a wooden ball, which felt the same shape. Further, she was persuaded to 'post' it through the top of a bucket with a hole in the lid. In this way she began to let go of an object she wanted and retrieve it with my encouragement. She began to get involved with something outside herself. ■

**What are we trying to do?**

Getting in touch with some people can be very difficult because of their sensory and cognitive losses, their perceptual difficulties and, in some, their fear, anger, confusion and withdrawal. We are looking for something that interests them so much that they respond, and looking to see how this can be built into an activity we can share. The sort of questions we should be asking are:

*What exactly is this person doing?*

Responses should always be non-judgmental. For example, it is easy to exclude reference to those behaviours that we may believe people ought not to be doing, such as self-abusing or apparently purposeless and circular activities.

It is essential to try to understand what the behaviour is doing. We should bear in mind that our behaviours help us to deal with our worlds.

*How can we build the experiences people are giving themselves into an enabling process that will help us to communicate with each other?*

- The woman who is blind kicks furniture to know where she and it are — a sort of echo-sounding system. She became more responsive when support workers ceased to view this as challenging and stamped as they walked. She knew where they were.

- A woman who hit her cheek and rendered her skin raw, responded to me tapping my own cheek in the same rhythm. She started to watch and then varied her own routines to see if I was following her. This led to her becoming more interactive with her own staff as they worked with her in the same way.

- A man who was only interested in manipulating a lump of wood with a hole would not eat from a spoon or even hold one. I made it easier for him to do so by giving him a wooden kitchen spoon with a hole drilled through it.

*When you have claimed a person's attention, what then?*

The principal aim of the interventions described in this and previous sections is to claim people's attention, so that we can start to relate to each other in a way which is mutually enabling.

Presenting experiences in compelling forms, either directly or indirectly, opens new ways of relating to people and the world outside that in which they have previously been locked. The experiences they once enjoyed in repetitive and self-stimulating forms can become a vehicle for exchange.

### What about people who find face-to-face interactions too threatening?

It is possible to devise alternative ways of working with people by:

- looking away and using indirect speech (see **Narrative 26**, **Paula**)

- shifting the focus of attention away from face-to-face confrontation and directing it into an activity which the person finds stimulating. This can be done both by 'infiltrating' repetitive behaviours such as scratching the hand (**Narrative 5**, **Roger**), or rocking (**Narrative 7**, **Kate**), or working through fixations on external objects (**Narrative 10**, **Rodney** with his 'spinners' and **Narrative 15**, **Peter**, rotating objects)

- working through a transparent screen (**Narrative 17**, **Jack**)

- giving a person more space (**Narrative 12**, **George**).

**Pat** (**Narrative 23**) seemed to use speech as a way of protecting herself. She was uninterested in distracting alternatives. If attempts persisted, she became very distressed. When the mode of intervention was switched from verbal to visual, using the images of her stereotype, her defensive reactions and distress ceased. Her attention was caught and the student and she were able to work together in a creative way. In turn, Pat began to use speech more relevantly.

### How can you connect with people using equipment?

The activities and equipment to which we introduce people are only effective if they are connected to recognisable patterns, rather than requiring people to take part in or be peripheral to activities which they tolerate but which have no meaning for them.

It will be recalled that **John** (**Narrative 1**) tolerated the schedule of activities that his support staff had devised for him but it was not until they found ways of catching his attention that he started to relate to them and they to him in a personal way. They shared his pleasure when he laughed and responded to the bottle rolling to and fro across the table. Shared laughter makes it possible to see people in a positive way. They had found one way of speaking John's language.

The importance of an activity being connected to a pattern with which a person is familiar and finds interesting was made very plain in working with **Rodney** (**Narrative 10**) who loved spinning objects. He had responded well to a box full of these and worked quietly and creatively with them and with us for a period of about twenty minutes. When he returned to his room, he was taken to sit down and told to, 'Make a card because you haven't done it yet.' He immediately became upset at the request as it had no meaning for him.

### Difficulties to be overcome

Although people with complex support needs require different and occasional extraordinary support, they often receive this from **untrained staff** for whom practical hands-on training is rarely available. This leaves staff unequal to answering such questions as, 'What shall we do with Pete today?' or 'What shall we try next?'

So-called challenging behaviour may be made worse by activities that most of us take for granted — shopping in a supermarket, for example. Exposing individuals with acute anxiety or perceptual disabilities to a noisy and **apparently disordered environment** may be extremely distressing, especially if they are unable to rely on information coming from their senses.

Further, the eye-contact we take for granted, may be painful for some people described as having 'autistic tendencies' but these people can relate if direct gaze and speech are avoided.

At review meetings to discuss individual programmes, staff will often frame service supports as needs, 'She needs to clean her teeth … dress herself…' and so on. Such statements may be true but they ignore the overwhelming need of all of us to feel loved and valued. Reference only to an unchanging and unvaried listing of self-help skills is an effective means of being disengaged from what matters in all our lives. Skills training should start with one question:

### How can teaching this skill enhance this person's feeling of self-worth?

A house leader said, 'Our service is so involved with what people can do, that we haven't been thinking about what they feel.' Most often, emphasis is placed on teaching actual skills, and to this end, programmes are carried out with varying degrees of success. Problems arise when teaching skills is seen as the only goal or indeed when staff are impatient to witness further changes. It is easier to teach someone than to 'be with' them. But attentiveness is vital in establishing communication with people who are severely withdrawn, attentiveness to exactly what this person is doing now, what their behaviour is eloquently communicating. We all too often try to impose our own solutions and refuse to learn from abject failure. As a speech therapist involved in this work said: 'I have to learn to listen to them through their communication, not mine.'

Moving to the long term, it appears that an initial rapid improvement may be followed by a plateau where there is no continuing

progress. There are a number of possibilities to be considered here.

- The person may have reached a limit at this stage of development.

- The person may need time to assimilate the new experiences before moving on.

- Environmental and human factors such as lack of space, poor design and layout and patterns of care may impose partial limits on the person's development.

- Continuity is an essential element of person-centred work. One woman who was introduced to a programme of work experienced a discontinuity of staff which resulted in a return to her self-stimulatory patterns and withdrawal. Further, it is important that any method of intervention that is chosen is not dependent on the personality of a support worker. Skills should be transferable to all members of a support team.

- Because this way of working is **a means whereby two people can relate** rather than a way of teaching a skill, we should not be in too much of a hurry to find alternative ways of intervention. Getting the pace right is very important. Although we need to be sensitive to the variations that the other person introduces and also to introduce our own gradually, it is important to identify an acceptable pace. It is usually quite obvious when people are ready to move on.

- The length of sessions needs to be thought out, taking into consideration what support staff can manage. Many interventions with people with profound disabilities are too long. We need to find out what individuals can tolerate. Working together for short periods more frequently, perhaps a few minutes several times a day, may prevent overloading people. It is useful to try and tie the time of an intervention to some recognisable feature of the day, such as after a meal or a bath, so that they can begin to anticipate.

Finally, it is rare that the support of people with complex needs aspires to enriching their lives. Rather, reducing the demands they make on their families and support workers is an explicit goal. Different disciplines claim responsibility for different domains: for example, gross and fine motor development is the responsibility of the physiotherapist, speech and communication of the speech therapist. Non-ambulatory, non-toilet-trained and non-verbal men and women do not generally evoke a holistic approach to their service needs. The universe of skills associated with communication and its expanding limits are too important to be reduced to a piecemeal subject speciality with narrow curriculum objectives.

# Section Six

# The Individual-Led Approach: How Well Does It Work?

The narratives presented in earlier sections show that individuals formerly seen as residing in their 'own world' can learn to interact and become less isolated. In turn, people's support personnel and families view them differently and become more confident in exploring different ways of securing their attention. This is illustrated further in the narrative below.

### 34. Reg

Reg is in his thirties. He has severe learning disabilities, visual impairment and partial hearing loss. He also has severe epilepsy. Reg lives on a farm. He attends a day centre for people with special needs. They find it difficult that he likes to wander round and will not sit down and join in group activities. If made to sit down, Reg tends to drift off to sleep which upsets his nocturnal sleeping pattern. It is very easy for him to slip into a cycle of disturbed sleep and severe fits.

Reg's mother said that he liked looking at checks, such as on a draught board, and through grids or perforated utensils such as colanders or sieves. We made him a number of pieces of equipment based on these patterns. When his mother showed these to him, they were able to sit down and work together for a whole evening. She said that it was the first time she had been able to make something to which he responded and she wished she had realised the value of

focused and engaging activities for him years ago. She added that the things had added 'fun' to his life and a positive dimension to their relationship. ■

The sum of the preceding narratives captures the different degrees of changes that resulted from person-centred interventions. Some of the views and reactions of support personnel to new ways of working are presented below. They all had a lot of experience of working with people with challenging behaviour and severe sensory loss.

It should be recalled that the people who have been described were those for whom the efforts of support staff had yielded little. It was believed they were beyond the reach of communication and relationships. For the great majority, support workers report that they 'no longer feel cut off'. They report feeling 'more confident' that they will be able to find ways of working with individuals.

- 'I feel quite differently about him now, much closer.'

- 'I feel very moved by the response I am getting.'

- 'Finding out what a person responds to and building up a friendly relationship is very important. When you do find that link and you see the person warm to you and a glimmer of hope in their eyes, you have a great sense of communication.'

- 'It (the course) made me realise that quite often, although we say we treat our clients as individuals, we miss out on one key area ... and that is we do not get to know our clients on a personal inner level. We quite often ignore feelings by not recognising their communications and communicating with them in their own way.'

- 'I saw the client in a new way, I had met her on a different level of understanding. I know now that I have the ability to help her reach a better quality of life.'

Talking about some equipment for a man who was blind and receiving no sensory input as he always managed to break things:

- 'The delight on his face was a moment to be savoured — he could not be parted from his new, workable world.'

A speech therapist reports on:

- 'the gratifying level of success achieved in such a short period of time (about three weeks). One lady responded far more during the course than had been achieved in the past two years of intervention. As a result, support staff are viewing this lady in a very different way and although sceptical at first and wary of feeling 'silly and awkward', are now totally committed to continuing the work. They feel at last, that they are beginning to communicate with her and as a result feeling a true bonding with her. They also feel they are working realistically and feel an enormous sense of pleasure at being able to work *with* her.'

In one district, the way of working described above (see page 5) as Intensive Interaction, was tried with six people. All showed an immediate positive response. Three months later, the four who were ambulant and could therefore carry out what they wanted to do, were described as 'reacting more positively to their surroundings and were more aware of people, relating not only passively as receivers but initiating contact themselves'.

# Section Seven
## Equipment and Materials

### Designing equipment

When designing equipment, the following questions should be asked:

- What is the experience a person is giving themselves, perhaps to the exclusion of other people and their environment?

- Is there a way in which the use of equipment will make it possible to engage the attention of someone for whom a direct approach is too threatening?

- Would it add variety and be more interesting if we incorporated this stimulus into a piece of equipment they might enjoy by reaching out to explore?

- What is the best way of presenting this?

- Does the design need to meet other requirements such as trying to facilitate particular movements through an enjoyable activity?

- How can we design the equipment so that it addresses the limitations of physical or sensory disabilities?

- What materials best meet the requirements of such factors of robustness, weight, position, availability, attractiveness, ease of handling, cleaning and safety?

### Using equipment

The use of equipment should not be regarded as an end in itself.

Any programme or equipment designed for an individual is used for very specific purposes:

- **To provide a new stimulus to encourage a response.**

David (**Narrative 2**) responded to activities and equipment based on his finger movements.

- **To encourage particular movements.**

Steve (**Narrative 18**) learned to turn his head and scan on the side where he had no sight. Gary (**Narrative 4**) learned to hold on to a corrugated tube he liked the feel of, using both his hands and stretching his arms.

- **To help people to express strong emotions.**

This can be facilitated by the use of games and through drawing. **Ron (Narrative 25)** was able to talk about the anger that was triggering his outbursts. **Pat (Narrative 23)** made use of the board with acetates and photographs of the 'figures' around which her repetitive speech patterns revolved to release some of her anger.

- **To develop communication.**

Mike (**Narrative 19**), who found it difficult to learn sign language, accepted the use of palm-sized wooden letters so that his support workers could communicate with him.

- **To provide enjoyment for an individual based on activities and things they like.**

Reg's mother (**Narrative 34**) said that the things she made for him provided him with endless pleasure as he examined them and looked at other things through them. She said they reminded her of 'other men's hobbies'.

- **To provide an enjoyable activity which can be shared.**

Jim (**Narrative 30**) enjoyed making his box and he started using relevant speech.

## Range of equipment

It is often not possible to buy sensory equipment suitable for the unique and diverse needs of people who are not responding to ordinary stimuli.

The equipment described in this report is normally made of:

- plywood
- plastic such as Styrene, particularly Styrene mirror
- Foamex, a compressed plastic in bright attractive colours, or
- polycarbonate, a substitute for glass that does not shatter like acrylic plastics.

These diverse materials satisfy the requirements of being cheap, robust and easy to manipulate. The resulting equipment satisfies the twin requirements of being precisely tailored to the needs of the individual and safe to use.

Many people described in this report had little or no sight, so it is not surprising that quite a large proportion of the equipment made for and with them was tactile. Different textures were used, especially Astroturf which has a springing, scratchy feel. For those with physical disability, particular attention had to be paid to positioning so that the stimulatory surface was in a position where it could be reached. For a number of people it was necessary to design extended or adapted tables to fit wheelchairs. Commercially available tables tend to be very narrow, not large enough to accommodate equipment, especially if a person pushes things round before managing to grasp them.

It will be recalled that the accordion was used in interventions with a number of people. It has a wide range of frequencies and so is helpful with people with auditory impairment who may only be able to hear a limited range of notes. It vibrates and moves as it plays and many people find it fascinating — much more interesting than a keyboard. It is the ideal instrument for interactive work, especially a 'student' model as it is not heavy and cumbersome. It is not necessary to be able to 'play' the instrument.

# Conclusion

Donna Williams[6] says:

> 'If you learn to speak their language you may just be able to reach them.'

The programme of work which has been the subject of this report hinged on learning to identify and use the languages of people whose often extreme extra support needs have excluded them from ordinary interactions and shared activities.

Key aspects of the work are:

- hearing from support personnel about individuals

- seeking to establish a helpful way of attracting an individual's attention

- using stimuli which are familiar to the individual

- presenting the stimulus which engages the person in ever-more-fascinating forms, perhaps by designing personalised equipment or 'games'

- exploring with support personnel and line managers ways in which work with individuals might be sustained.

Although the 60 support staff who contributed to the work described in this report were selected on the basis of motivation rather than their creative skills, it was possible to encourage them to regard people's behaviours as language and to reconsider ways in which they might communicate with them. Further, it was possible to teach most of them ways of designing and building simple equipment. Many reflected that they found these creative approaches mutually transforming.

These ways of working with support personnel, in order to effect significant and positive changes in the lives of people formerly perceived as challenging and isolated, offer a lot of promise. The challenge now is for service providers to sustain their investment in more person-centred approaches.

# References

1. Wertheimer, A. (1995) *Reaching Out. Skills and Development Therapy with People with Severe Learning Disabilities.* SENSE.

2. Ephraim, G. W. (1986) *A Brief Introduction to Augmented Mothering.* Playtrack Pamphlet, Harperbury Hospital, Radlett, Herts.

3. Nind and Hewett (1994) *Access to Communication.* David Fulton Press.

4. Birath, G. (1991) Private communication.

5. Williams, D. (1992) *Nobody Nowhere.* London: Doubleday.

6. Williams, D. Videotaped Interview, NBC.

**Contact address**

Phoebe Caldwell
c/o Norah Fry Research Centre
3 Priory Road
Bristol
BS8 1TX